Innovative Online Solutions
Free Effective Business Strategies

By:

David K. Ewen, M.Ed.

Ewen Prime Company

Forest Academy

ISBN-13: 978-1515067344
ISBN-10: 1515067343

Innovative Online Solutions

Free Effective Business Strategies

By:

David K. Ewen, M.Ed.

Ewen Prime Company

Forest Academy

Dedication

We all have gifts that we appreciate and can offer solutions to other people. It is wonderful when we have the skills an talent to do good things for people. Everyone's ability and skills come from a calling from God to put to good use. It is honed with experience, education, training, practice, and guidance.

I dedicate this book, first to my father Doc Ewen (Dr. Harold I. Ewen) who purchased my first computer when I was in High School. It was not common in 1981 for a teenager to explore digital technology and see the future. As the discoverer of the existence of Hydrogen Line in space, he knows best of being innovative and looking to the future.

Secondly, I would like to dedicate this book to my beautiful wife Maria. She teaches me and others around her of the word "love" and its meaning. Part of that comes from a passion to be the best that you can be. With the help of my wife, I have been able to explore passions and be the best that I am.

Next, I would like to dedicate this book to my Pastors. Pastor Jose Martinez and Pastor Melly Martinez of the Resurrection Center have taught me that our best talents originate from God and that the Glory be to God for all that we do. As part of the covering of the Resurrection Center, I would also give great thanks and loving appreciation to Apostle Enrique Narvaez and Apostle Lourdes Narvaez.

After finding true Christianity with Open Gate Ministries with Pastor Mike Trazinski, Pastor Colette Trazinski, Pastor Martia Manchester, and Pastor Barry Manchester, I have been able to explore the true meaning of life in ways that I never thought possible. It is from there, I expanded exploration of God's purpose for me when I became one of the many incredible people to help build the Resurrection Center.

My greatest dedication of course goes to God who has given to me all that I have. He has provided the protection, the education, the nurturing, and my development to reach toward the calling He has for me.

David K. Ewen, M.Ed.

July 2015

About the Author

David K. Ewen, M.Ed. is an author, speaker, and talk show host. He is the managing editor of EPN News. His lecture tours include digital multimedia technologies that include website and mobile app development. He is an author of numerous books on technologies, business, communications, and computer applications. This book is the culmination of years' experience in website and mobile app development that eventually evolved into part of a three-hour lecture conference to train individuals on the topic. This subject is part of the "Professor Lecture Series" that is held in the seven states of New York and New England. The series began in June 2004 in Massachusetts and has spread to New York and all of New England. In addition to Websites and mobile apps development, other courses in computer technology are included as part of the "Professor Lecture Series". They include among others, Excel, PowerPoint, Blogging, Windows 8, and QuickBooks. Some other technical topics include publishing, broadcasting, recording, and other digital multimedia technologies. Ten years before the "Professor Lecture Series" was launched, Ewen Prime Company was launched as a book-publishing house. That was in 1994. After that, broadcasting on WORC 1310 AM & WGFP 940 AM began what would the beginning of a broadcasting career and the start of the EPN network and EPN NEWS. With a variety of media, technology, and communications experience, the author

David K. Ewen, M.Ed. shares his experience through Lectures that are face-to-face an online as well as a variety of content in print, Recorded, and on video.

David K. Ewen, M.Ed. as an Online Broadcaster

David K. Ewen, M.Ed. has been a broadcast journalist and radio talk show host since 1998. He is the anchor of Education World News and managing editor or Your World Discovered. David's first broadcast was from the twin towers of hot-talk WORC 1310 AM and WGFP 940 AM on a weekly LIVE morning show in New England.   David has also been very much involved with community access television broadcasting and film production. David is one of the original hosts of Blog Talk Radio with his first broadcast in April 2007. In 2009, he launched five radio shows for Circle of Seven Productions to increase that company's reach to consumers. He is the host of Today's Author, Education World News, and Your World Discoverd. The shows are syndicated on five mobile app networks that include Blog Talk Radio, Stitcher, TuneIn, iTunes, and Blubrry. The shows are broadcasted LIVE and saved as podcasts.

<u>Introduction</u>

I love what technology has done for people and how it has made the world smaller. Every year, innovations are released making computers, mobile devices, and other technologies used in ways to more quickly evolve our ways to communicate. Some say there is an information overflow. As a boy, there were three TV channels available. Now there are so many, I do not know how many are available. But that's just TV. What about the content on other mediums? This accelerated pace of innovation has made it hard for some people to keep up. I've made it a career to keep up with the technology and help other keep up to.

As a professor of digital multimedia technologies, I always have to be on top of my game when it comes to online technologies. My lectures are three-hour workshop seminars with a wide range of people from different demographics. This book is for people looking to get an insight on how today's online technology is used. You will also find strategies and resources that are relevant to today's emerging online environment.

My original career after college was as a systems programmer for mainframe computers. After fifteen years, I went on to launch a business in book publishing. Book publishing began with creating products that were pretty looking on a bookshelf. Eventually ebooks emerged turning book publishing from creating products that looked pretty on a shelf to those that are easily distributed on the web. Once that happened, I was able to say, "Now they're talking my language."

The technical changes in book publishing evolved my career into film, record albums, broadcasting, journalism and more. Eventually, I became a professor of digital multimedia technologies working on a variety of media platforms. In addition to creating the content, I took the publicity experience in book publishing and applied it to other media venues, with of course, significant development.

As of the writing of this book (July 2015), I broadcast nearly every day for hours at a time from the USA to Japan as a conference education environment. My global experience began before by becoming one of the original talk show hosts on Blog Talk Radio. A variety of other individual business opportunities has taken me online to work with India, Canada, Australia, and the UK. Today's technology enables us to travel around the world.

My work as the managing editor of EPN News and Your World Discovered encourages me to share how online writing evolves. This book includes elements of copywriting.

Content

- Business Succeed With Online Advertising
- Effective Writing Made Easy
- Getting The Best Results from YouTube
- How Quality Content Can Improve Income from AdSense
- How To Make an Online Store Effective
- Important and Effective Ecommerce Strategies
- Improving Facebook Effectiveness for Business
- Making E-books An Effective Online Product
- Making Money Online with Honest Effort
- Making Twitter Effective For Marketing
- Managing Free Giveaways to Consumers
- Selling Educational Products to Consumers
- Succeeding with Affiliate Marketing
- The Evolution of Online Tutoring and Coaching
- What Makes an Ebook Sell?

Business Succeed With Online Advertising

Businesses that use display advertising learn that there are two business models. One called CPC or Cost per Click involves paying for activity to a posted ad. The other called CPA or Cost per Action involves paying a commission or royalty for a product sold. CPA falls under affiliate marketing category of display advertising where an affiliate sells products or services on the business's behalf and pays a commission for every online sale. CPC or Cost per Click falls under the category of traditional online advertising. CPC results in a passive stream of revenue based on referrals to a product, service, or website found on the web. CPA has greater revenue potential as affiliates make efforts to sell the product or service directly to online consumers.

Businesses appreciate the low risk investment of online advertising. Payment applies only if either activity shows on CPC activity or something sells when using CPA advertising. Businesses use Google's AdWords as the most common advertising platform appreciated. Content publishers use Google AdSense to post advertising based on genre on their website, blog, or online publication. Google's advertising engine works with two platforms; AdWords and AdSense. Together they help advertisers generate responses and content owners generate revenue. Another advertising platform "Advertising" continues to show continued success for both advertisers and content owners.

Google's Analytics platform offers the ability to track advertising activity. Businesses use the reporting features of Google Analytics to boost sales and find more visitors. There reporting works for mobile apps too, for example the ads submitted on ADmob from Google.

Affiliate marketing continues to grow as one of the more lucrative revenue generating units for a business. As more affiliate opportunities grow, businesses can rely on other digital content owners to market and sell their products and services. Rakuten, formally LinkShare, provides one of the most popular affiliate marketing platforms. CJ Affiliate by Conversant, formally called Commission Junction, continues to be a strong competitor against Rakuten. Businesses use Rakuten, CJ Affiliate, and others to spread opportunity. Smaller businesses take advantage of Click Bank to sell digital products directly to the consumer.

Effective Writing Made Easy

Writers often wonder what to write. The confusion comes from trying to figure out what each paragraph should look like rather than the point made. The mistake writers make involves thinking and writing at the same time when developing a written piece of work. Thinking and writing do not happen in the same way and avoided when developing thought and written content.

The challenges from writing an article come from how best to organize thoughts. Creating content seems effortless as long as the right process is used. Often writers start from the beginning and continue to the end resulting in confused thoughts. Writing from thinking fails because thoughts are developmental and not complete. Written content needs organization and completeness. Developmental thoughts used in writing have no organization and lacks completeness.

A clean process to write effectively involves organizing content backwards. That means starting from the concluding end of the article and work backward to the starting introduction. This may not be the most natural way of writing, but helps align thinking with writing. Fast moving thoughts work operate with desire and then how to get there. That means working with a conclusion and then figuring out the introduction. This writing style begins with the conclusion written first and the introduction written last. The result moves the paragraphs in the right order.

Because thought process operates on desires and therefore conclusion, written content developed first with a conclusion is more intuitive with the thinking process. When writing the conclusion, steps leading to the conclusion do not need to consideration until later. Having an effective, powerful, meaningful conclusion has the greatest importance for written content. That conclusion serves as the lasting impact vehicle for the reader. That impactful message remains lasting.

The body of the content involves a list of points that lead to the conclusion. This bulleted list creates the path toward the conclusion. For each bulleted list, three or more sentences make up the paragraph. The final part written is also the first part that is read by the audience. The introduction serves as an opening to the points made in the body of the content. After writing all elements, the obvious title is apparent. It should consist of four to five words at best.

Getting The Best Results from YouTube

YouTube evolved into one of the greatest video sharing sites people know. It has become the second largest search engine second to Google. And Google owns <u>YouTube</u>. The platform maintains its strength by having a powerful developer and search engine behind it. As a social media sight, YouTube enjoys the same popularity and uniqueness as Facebook. A monstrous number of hours of content upload every day. With the evolution of smartphones, varieties of candid and on the spot videos find their way to YouTube. Simple free video editors like <u>iMovie</u> and <u>Windows Movie Maker</u> has increased in popularity with the growth of YouTube. Any major producer of movies or product developer for a company has a trailer or promo video online. When people want to learn something, they go to YouTube to learn how.

Anyone can take hold of the power YouTube gives web marketers and businesses. The <u>monetization</u> of YouTube videos generates revenue for businesses. With a variety of ad options that include embedding, banners, and more, people enjoy a greater chance of generating <u>revenue</u> with YouTube. Content on YouTube crowds and camouflages the good content. People needing improved representation on YouTube must do more for greater recognition. Many views on YouTube involve a search for the content owner. A good profile provides interest to other videos uploaded by the same user. One good video generates leads to other videos this way. A YouTube channel offers the ability to have a trailer that entices visitors to see more and visit often. The profile must include a good profile picture and description. Visitors look for detail from authors of incredible videos. The primary channel page introduced on Facebook or Twitter drives social media traffic to YouTube videos. The general online visitor has attraction to videos.

With today's evolving technologies even on the smart device people carry, the necessity of videos in high definition with crisp sound had greater importance. Although smartphones have good quality, a quality camera that does better with picture and sound makes videos more enticing and attractive. These cameras have external condenser directional mics for a crisp amplified sound. The requirements include well-lit images, at least thirty frames per second, sound recorded at 44.1K KHz with no less than 16 bit PCM. The sound density sounds more natural with an analog sound at the common 192 bit PCM. To give that professional TV sound, the removal of white noise provides a professional sound. A great free tool for sound editing comes from Audacity from Sourceforge

How Quality Content Can Improve Income from AdSense

The money earning capability of Google AdSense on websites and blogs depends on the content on those platforms. Advertisement only works with sufficient consumer traffic who responds to ads. This concept remains true beginning back in the days of newspaper delivery and radio broadcasting. Back then, effective return on investment of advertising required sufficient distribution of content. The ad responders resulted in a small percentage of the entire distribution population. Quality content continues to have importance on content quality for distribution. Without quality, consumers direct themselves to other resources. The content with the best distribution and access tends to do well with getting a return on investment of advertising money.

A first time visitor to a website has one opportunity to have a good impression. Websites do not have second chances for a first impression. That first impression must be good. This involves effective, engaging, quality content. AdSense from Google works with high traffic. Ads show on high traffic websites. Repeat website visitors increase the likelihood of ad responses that convert to residual income for the website owner.

The abundance of tools to create articles includes resourced searched under "Article Template." Many free resources guide writers on how to build titles, topics, and generating content. The reading audience of today looks for informative content that wets the appetite to come back for more. All content should remain consistent with the theme of the website. This ensures a unique audience with related ads fitting closer to the needs of the audience. This improves effectiveness of ads and the passive revenue that generates overtime.

A time consuming element that website owners tend to shy away from is writing sufficient content. Web visitors look for content no less than 400 words. Anything less has reduced value and little relevance to the consumer's needs. Writing an article with substance at 250 words fails to be complete for what the reading audience looks for. The style of writing improves by eliminating passive voice verbs such as be, is, are, a, was, were. Word processing platforms such MS Word highlights passive voice content to be resolved. By putting attention on quality content and some useful tricks to drive traffic, the ads placed on websites and blogs can provide good residual income.

How To Make an Online Store Effective

A successful internet based business has automation built in so that income is residual and passive. This means the onetime setup of the business results in ongoing income. The early forms of internet businesses required daily maintenance that took time. Today, internet businesses work by themselves while business owners conduct additional business operations to make income. The technology available today allows for automation of income generation. The most successful internet businesses have high volume traffic and accommodate sales for that traffic.

The storefront built includes a domain name pointed to a URL (built website) with effective SEO (Search Engine Optimization) making it findable. Social Media Optimization (SMO) ensures the website has strong representation in high traffic social media sights such as Facebook, Twitter, and many others. Any digital products sold on the website do not need shipping and have instant delivery to the consumer. Popular digital products include e-books, online classes, and software. The genre of product should be specialized to make selling easier and more effective to reach a consumer population.

As part of automating websites, purchases made through PayPal or other online payments system satisfies 24x7 service. Consumers make purchases with the websites' ability to highlight the product. Descriptions, pictures, videos, and downloadable PDFs on the website satisfy the consumer's appetite for knowledge about products. Sellers must put great attention into the detail of that descriptive content so that the consumer fully understands the product purchased. Consumers only buy when the product satisfies a need or want and they fully understand what the product offers.

The most successful online stores have high consumer traffic. This means the website syndication includes blogs, forums, social media, email distribution, and more. A website resident online does not mean products sell. The hardest parts of selling products online consist of getting enough consumer traffic and having sufficient descriptive material for the product. By satisfying those needs, online sales can grow.

Today's ecommerce environment consists of a collection of genres with online store specializing in those genres. Effective online sellers specialize in products because they specialize in a particular customer's needs. This means the seller understands the buyer and their needs.

Important and Effective Ecommerce Strategies

In the age of digital technology and a growing internet world, many people flock to the business arena that the web offers. It is attractive 'work-at-home' style of revenue has enticed many people to start an online business. What those people have not thought about, is that they crowd a growing market of online entrepreneurs making ecommerce a crowded mall. Necessary steps make online businesses successful if planned correctly. Simple efforts and sufficient time will create an online business that works. Some basic elements necessary for online businesses can easily go forgotten. This results in a cost in ecommerce development due to the waste of online inactivity.

Products and services sold online need a website to serve as a storefront. Websites alone will not make a person's ecommerce efforts successful overnight. Many available DYI or 'do-it-yourself' website development tools help create a fantastic professional looking website. These free tools need only a domain name. A domain name forwards the search to the URL built with the DYI site. The list of good candidates for DYI website building includes WordPress, Wix, Weebly, webs and more.

The physical buying need online purchase controls such as PayPal. This site offers HTML-embed code to put buy buttons on a website or blog. These buttons are to submit money for purchases, donations, and setting up recurring payments. Some DYI website building tools use PayPal as a default ecommerce option. Along with the purchase button from PayPal, a picture should be included as a showcase of the product or service made available

A website with PayPal partially solves the problem of creating an effective ecommerce environment. A vehicle to generate trust between seller and buyer creates an effective ecommerce environment. This involves contact information such as email and, if relevant, shipping address for returns. Google voice provides free phone numbers used to store voice mails from customers. Direct contact online using Skype gives a personal one-to-one connection that is more personal.

The glue that holds the whole ecommerce environment together is the descriptive content that describes the online store, products, services, and conditions. Any possible and potential question has an answer on the website. Often ecommerce sites take advantage of FAQ's (Frequently Asked Questions) as a way to pull all possible questions and associated answers together. Product and service descriptions along with pictures ensure the customer knows what they are buying.

The last part needed in ecommerce involves driving customer traffic. The two ways include free options and paid options. The free options require legwork. The paid options require someone else legwork and automated functions. Automated tools include social media distributors such as HootSuite and TweetDeck.

Improving Facebook Effectiveness for Business

Many years ago, the phrase internet highway meant businesses putting websites on the internet. Today, in many ways, those websites represent the back alleys and the high volume activity of social media represents a much faster, visible, increased volume that represents today's internet highway. With so much traffic on social media, managing its effectiveness has become important. Simply having a social media, presence does not satisfy the true effectiveness of what social media can offer. Businesses work to use social media for increasing traffic to ecommerce purchase points via websites or affiliate marketing platforms.

Facebook's traffic makes business representation much more difficult than the early founding of businesses on social media. Spam and nonsense content crowds the social media environment making it harder for consumers to notice businesses. Many businesses resort to paying for promoted posts and advertising. Often that route does not have the desired return on investment or long term residual customer contact growth. The investment of promoted posts and advertising supplements the currently reducing trend of organic views. Fortunately, businesses have opportunity to take advantage of smart techniques to increase views to improve social media performance effectiveness.

Today, many businesses use advertising that encourages consumers to LIKE and SHARE a Facebook page. This gets consumers connected to the business on Facebook. Many businesses discover that their social media audience increase overtime as the effort to suggest LIKES and SHARES on their page. Consumers tend to follow trends of other consumers and will like or share pages that their friends like and share. Continued exponential growth through LIKES and SHARES perpetuated by friends watching their friends do the same thing. This approach works effectively after sufficient likes and shares acquires growth.

More tools allow consumer to participate in a business's Facebook page. Surveys, comment sharing, and accepting calendar invites act as a call to action. Businesses enjoy greater social media effectiveness when they posts have calls to action and do more than provide content through posts. This interaction of the business and consumer increases a partnership of knowledge and trust of products and services that the business offers. The notion of expertise of a Facebook page improves integrity when business owners share it through forum posts.

Making E-books An Effective Online Product

Today's e-book market grows due to the popularity of digital content sold in book form. Selling books presents a profitable market as long as sufficient traffic from interested consumers exists. Many people use platforms such as SmashWords, ClickBank, CreateSpace, NookPress, and more to create book covers and e-published content. The resources to create the product have an abundant supply of tools and techniques. Unfortunately, due to easy publication of e-books, consumers find worthless reading online that they pay for. This makes consumer buying hesitant and making publishing and selling harder. Today, having quality content fails to be enough to satisfy the information hungry consumer. They want to know that a purchase has a trusted return on investment. That biggest challenge publishers have involves proving their content's worth.

Due to the trustworthiness of e-book content, increased consumer traffic flow to the content helps with sales numbers. A percentage of all traffic to an ecommerce product results in a sale. Some percentages result in poor sales due to insufficient traffic. A two percent buy rate, for example, is profitable or worthwhile only if sufficient consumer traffic reaches the content. Search Engine Optimization and Social Media Optimization play a big role in getting traffic to reach websites. Replicating social media posts using HootSuite or TweetDeck saves time and has proven effectiveness. A findable ecommerce sight relevant to common searches brings products directly to consumers.

Search Engine Optimization effectiveness changes as search engine owners such as Google make changes to their search algorithms. What works one year may not be as effective the following year. A one-time SEO set-up using effective HTML embed codes may not always have the best results. SEO has importance but not the sole solution to visibility. Other environments include collaboration that includes participation forums, online magazines, and eCommerce reviews. These ways consumers learn directly from the seller of products sold online. This provides an increased level of trust.

Traditional book marketing for e-books include the author tour. An example includes radio interviews on Blog Talk Radio. Look for shows syndicated on online radio apps such as Stitcher and TuneIn. These shows have a greater online distribution. The online show broadcasts LIVE and saved as a podcast shared on social media sights for added distribution.

Making Money Online with Honest Effort

Moneymaking strategies that involve selling a scheme to helps others make money online has mixed results and often disappointment. People who sell these products have not made money themselves yet. This makes it hard for the seller to show buyers how effective the product is because they cannot speak of it with experience. For many people wanting residual income online, selling products to help others make money often fails. It looks too much like untrusted multilevel marketing that in time will evolve to obsolescence. Sellers who

Many people try making money online and find frustration because of overhead effort. They work on creating a website and building a product. So much time is developing the online store, which time shrinks on bringing the product the online market. A struggle becomes greater with cut corners and shortcuts to bring products to market. Some people work with others in a joint venture. When not working in unity, the process fails. The hurt comes when there is a huge effort for failed results. This causes stress, anxiety, and disappointment. That does not have to happen. The right tools online when used correctly create success. Unfortunately, many tools offered online camouflage the real ones that work.

People buy products and services online when they have a feeling of trust from whom they believe serve as a model of integrity. A purchase succeeds through faith. That faith comes from the buyer and represents the integrity of the seller. That said, the seller must not fake content for products and services. Buyers want information and understanding. A faked presentation fails because it cannot continue. Once a question goes unanswered effectively, the integrity of the seller fails. A buyer cannot continue with a dialog with a seller if trust does not exist. The seller must have the mindset that their product or service sells to a wide market and that it has value to consumers. Not all consumers want what a seller has.

A product or service worth sharing sells effectively online. A seller cannot speak about proprietary product and services in a way that shows integrity, honesty, and authenticity. A seller can reach an audience by being sharing knowledge as a subject matter expert on forums. This develops trust that buyers look for when finding the right product or service. The question in buyers mind is whom can they trust? They also want to converse with the buyer that involves understanding offers, getting help, and addressing any problems. This consistent action done daily and persistently achieves results. That is how the doors of ecommerce open to buyers effectively. Every daily small success achieves great results.

Making Twitter Effective For Marketing

Facebook cannot be the only social media businesses use to communicate with consumers. Twitter's design has to do with connecting people to others that they do not know. Ergo, the Hashtag feature. The hashtag's design involves relating posts to trending topics. Businesses can identify high volume trending topics with www.HashTags.org to put their posts in the path of higher traffic. That alone will not suffice getting followers. Often businesses take advantage of Tweet Deck to schedule posts with pictures at opportune times with the scheduling feature. Tweet Deck's scheduling feature allows businesses to enter posts with pictures at any day and time in the future with no limitations. Other advance promotion options to increase post visibility involve Ads by Twitter that involves a financial cost.

In addition to Tweet Deck and Ads by Twitter, businesses connect with consumers by connecting with others by retweeting other posts, following other accounts, and sharing common hashtags in posts. A constant stream of communication builds followers on Twitter through a variety of means that primary captures through posting to common hashtags and retweeting. The content generated on Twitter must also have relevancy to others. Pictures must compliment posts for more effectiveness. Text alone tends to have significantly less results than posts that have pictures. Combining post with pictures using highly effective hashtags identified through Hashtags.org results in greater Twitter activity. Tweet Deck offers an increased level of activity by automating the scheduling of posts for easier distribution of content over a stretch of time. Other apps available online use Twitter effectively for business to reach consumers. Hoot Suite similar to Tweet Deck reaches out to consumers on a variety of social media platforms, including Twitter at the same time.

Because Twitter represents a microblog, many website developers use Twitter as a blog. Updates by cellphone to Twitter satisfy easy content development for the blog. A tab on the website labelled BLOG routes directly to the Twitter feed. Because of simple cellphone updates through a blog, the Twitter feed remains up to date with current information. The feed also contains content generated through Tweet Deck allowing for planning blog posts. As a blog and tab on a website, Twitter serves as a news stream of information that includes information updated by cellphone, posted automatically by Twee Deck, and contains pictures for increased content interest.

Managing Free Giveaways to Consumers

A way to increase sales involves effectively using giveaways as in incentive to buy for the consumer. Incentives come in the form of urgency and sampling. The urgency demonstrates a limitation that consumers have to buy. This means limited time or a limited amount available. The free giveaway shows what and opportunity lost. Some consumers get a free giveaway while others will not. That giveaway provides testimonials to other people about the quality of product demonstrated. If consumers know that free giveaways have limitations, then intuitively, they know that products sold have limitations too.

Effective businesses use giveaways to educate the consumer population of their products. The sale of products or consumables covers the cost of giveaways. A business should never lose money on giveaways. The pricing of products and consumables offered to the public factors in the price of the free giveaway. Before releasing products to the market, a business creates a price point bearable by the consumer market and factors in a certain quantity of giveaways. The giveaways consist of a sampling of the final product. This sampling educates the consumer of what they can have. A giveaway takes the place of displaying a product as if in a showcase.

Other types of giveaways include a full complete product. Not many consumers benefit from a complete free giveaway. A contest or raffle gives values of a free giveaway and demonstrates the full product to a consumer. Consumers who win and achieve a product through a contest tend to more likely share the excitement of a winning. This gives positive value to the product. A product given away free has no value. A product or content requires effort and exhibits greater appreciation by the consumer.

Other giveaways include a sampling of products so that consumers educate themselves on products available. The purpose of a sample collection serves to share the best products available. Often giveaway samples end up shared among consumers for a greater distribution. Consumers tend to share a collection sample of products and keep what they like best and give others away. Therefore, a sample collection distributes to a larger audience.

Selling Educational Products to Consumers

Online classes, books, and other information related digital products are favorable among consumers wanting to learn. These types of information hungry consumers like quality informative content. Unfortunately, poor content has found its way online making it harder for consumers to find good products and seller to reach interested consumers. Poor content available clouds good content in the forest of online digital media. Businesses selling digital products must work smarter to understand the consumer and demonstrate a recognized benefit to the consumer.

Consumers buy online digital content when they know the value of what they are getting is real. This means they trust what they are buying. That trust comes from online packaging just like packaging of consumables in a store. Digital online packaging comes in the form of descriptions, testimonials, video demonstration, consumer ratings, and more. These things help consumers make buying decisions. A description of the product and picture fail to entice consumers to buy.

Effective products sold to consumers have value to the consumer. This means the seller knew what the buyer wanted. An effective buyer and seller relationship involves the seller knowing what the general consumer wants and what the expected benefits are. The seller must demonstrate understanding of the buyer's wanted benefits and expectation of results. This will capture the interest of the buyer. Too often sellers make the mistake of not connecting the product benefits with the buyer's wants or needs.

To reach a greater audience, sellers promote products to variety of consumers. This involves understanding categories of people, which comes from understanding market geographic and consumer demographics. The product sold must fit the people buying it. Otherwise, a disconnected relationship between buyer and seller exists. Sellers fail often when they do not understand who their customer is. For example, the product must have a price and value of use for the consumer buying the product. Sellers only buy products that make sense, fits their ability to purchase, and satisfies a need or want.

The online content must have an organization designed to fit the needs of most consumers. People looking for online content desire an organized structure that follows a logical sequential path. This means the learning process makes sense, not confusing, and relevant to consumer's needs. If a consumer looking for educational content recognizes a good structure from the content, then it will likely satisfy their need.

Succeeding with Affiliate Marketing

Businesses choose between standard online advertising and affiliate marketing to generate revenue. Affiliate marketing provides a commission to online affiliates for products or services sold. An intermediary company pairs advertisers and online publication owners. Owners of website, blogs, and other online content, referred to as publishers, work to sell products and services with the expectation of earning a commission from each sales. Some popular affiliate marketing platforms include Rakuten, Click Bank, and CJ Affiliates.

Content owners such as owners of websites and blogs carefully select merchants who they work with. A lot depends on the commission rate as a lot of work goes into selling products and services online. Many businesses rely on affiliate marketing to outsource sales efforts to increase sales volume. The affiliates select products or services that have good commission and demonstrate some sense of sell-ability. Products that seem to sell poorly and offer low commission does not provide a good return on investment for the affiliate pushing the sale online. An affiliate will not sell something that they would not buy themselves. The product must have mainstream interest from the public to make sales efforts worth it.

Content owners serving as affiliates fall into a niche that has relevance to their website, blog, or online publication. The relevancy has great importance to the affiliate selling the product or service. Ads on a website not relevant to the website itself look out of place and forced. Visitors look for things on websites and ads are only effective if they show relevance to the website. The website and ad must fall into the same niche to look like they complement each other and meant to be together. Affiliate ads that look out of place have minimal response.

Not all affiliate marketing ads work. Some may offer challenging conditions for a sale to occur. The relevancy of the product or service may have lost mainstream interest. Whatever the case may be, some affiliate ads either do not work from the beginning or fade from being effectiveness over time. Either way, changing ads on occasion and in some cases frequently, offers the best results. Ads intended for one time use and last forever do not work. An initial success may result, but further success requires change and variety to eliminate staleness.

The Evolution of Online Tutoring and Coaching

People looking to start an online business may consider providing online coaching or tutoring to students. Business owners having content to share and information to teach can provide services to people wanting to learn a new skill, be certified, or improve education their children. Many consumers take advantage of online classes because of the lower cost, easier scheduling, and time saved. Many colleges and universities offer online classes for programs and degrees. Online training has evolved into a normal way of learning. Online business owners have an opportunity to enter into this market.

Online coaching and tutoring continues to grow as a business. Consumers appreciate saving time online to learn new things. Many have also directed their children toward online tutoring and coaching to get specialized skilled training. Online classes purchased individually or part of an entire program allows consumers to select based on their particular need. This allows structured training to fit to the consumer's needs and schedule availability. With those needs being satisfied, consumers have tended to register for online courses for themselves and or their children.

Today's internet resources provide convenience of online training, coaching, and tutoring. Many classes run asynchronously through automation while others have a LIVE teacher to interact. Students recognize progress through a structured set of learning confirmations through simple online examinations. This way, students appreciate receiving the full value of the course. The online instructors can measure effectively the students' progress. Many online teaching programs certify students in skills for their careers. Online classes tend to be successful due to their lower cost and convenience.

Parents place their children in specialized online tutoring and coaching programs so that regular school schedule is not effective. The online sessions run in conjunction with the normal school schedule. This way tutoring and coaching is an addition to the learning process and not an extra step causing a delay. Students receiving tutoring in a specialized subject tend to improve test scores and learning process. This added coaching helps with the overall learning process. Parents find that online tutoring has effective results worth the small investment.

A normal school schedule operates during the day, evening, and weekend on a structured schedule. Online coaching and tutoring sessions have a more flexible schedule that allows it to being part of an existing busy schedule. The convenience comes from no travel saving cost and time.

What Makes an Ebook Sell?

When people buy books, they look for books. When looking for information, they go online and search. An e-book has a hard time selling, because of its online origin. The value of information of an e-book must have greater importance than information found online. Marketing an e-book requires greater promotion that goes beyond sharing information. A consumer buying any book knows of its important relevance to their needs. They also know that the information in the book is not online and found only in book form.

Information online is free or purchased. An e-book on sale must demonstrate importance and relevancy to the consumer making it worth the purchase. With so much free content online, many consumers may assume purchasing information like an e-book may not be in their best interest. This makes selling e-books more difficult without the right selling tools in place. Online e-book sellers must treat their products just like paperback books sold in stores. A unique value of the product demonstrated to consumers has a greater chance of selling.

The URL of the e-book online must have SEO (Search Engine Optimization) for improved search results findings by the consumer. This same information must also have strong representation in social media. Years ago, the information highway was websites. Today, the high traffic collaboration between buyers and sellers include social media and search engines. Those resources direct consumers to websites with e-books.

Many e-books produced through Amazon's CreateSpace platorm, SmashWords, and NookPress do not need websites to be developed. Many consumers expect e-books sold on Amazon and Barnes & Noble or other online venues distributed by SmashWords. This allows e-book sellers to put more attention on marketing the e-book and less time hosting on a website. E-book sellers must focus on blogging, social media posting, and posting on forums to share the value of their product.

E-books on sale must have representation as any other book on sale including paperbacks in a store. Books sell through the attractiveness of the author's skills, distinctions, accolades, and expertise. This makes the information contained within the book more valuable. Books sell because of the author or owner of the content. That stands behind the product and provides authenticity for the material.

Innovative Online Solutions

Free Effective Business Strategies

By:

David K. Ewen, M.Ed.

Ewen Prime Company

Forest Academy

Copyright © 2015